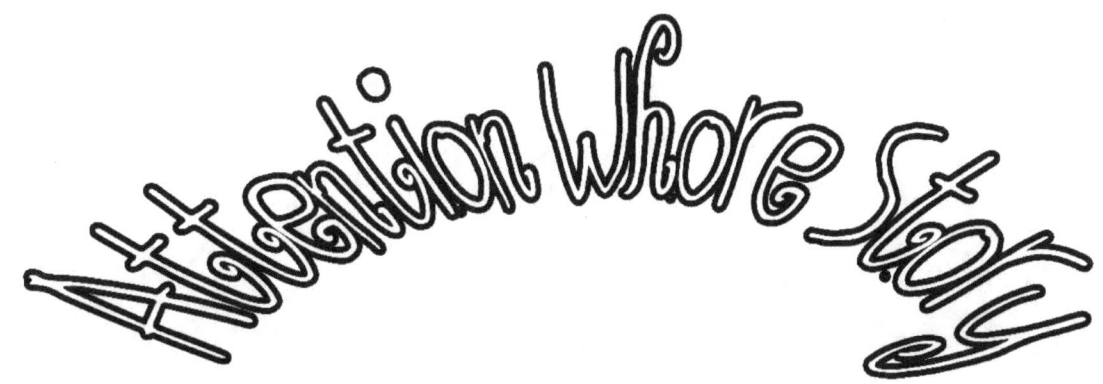

Attention Whore Story

Adorable Swear Word To Color

FOR STRESS RELEASING

By

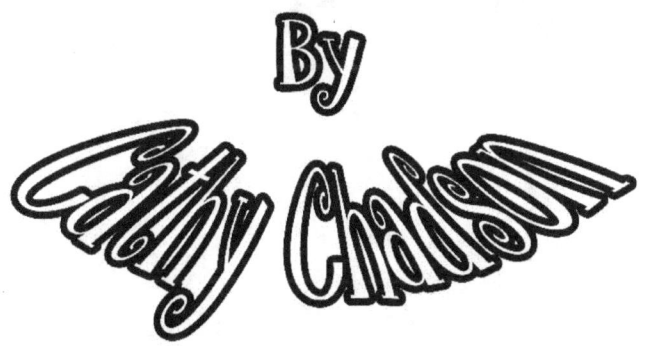

Cathy Chaisson

Happy Coloring!

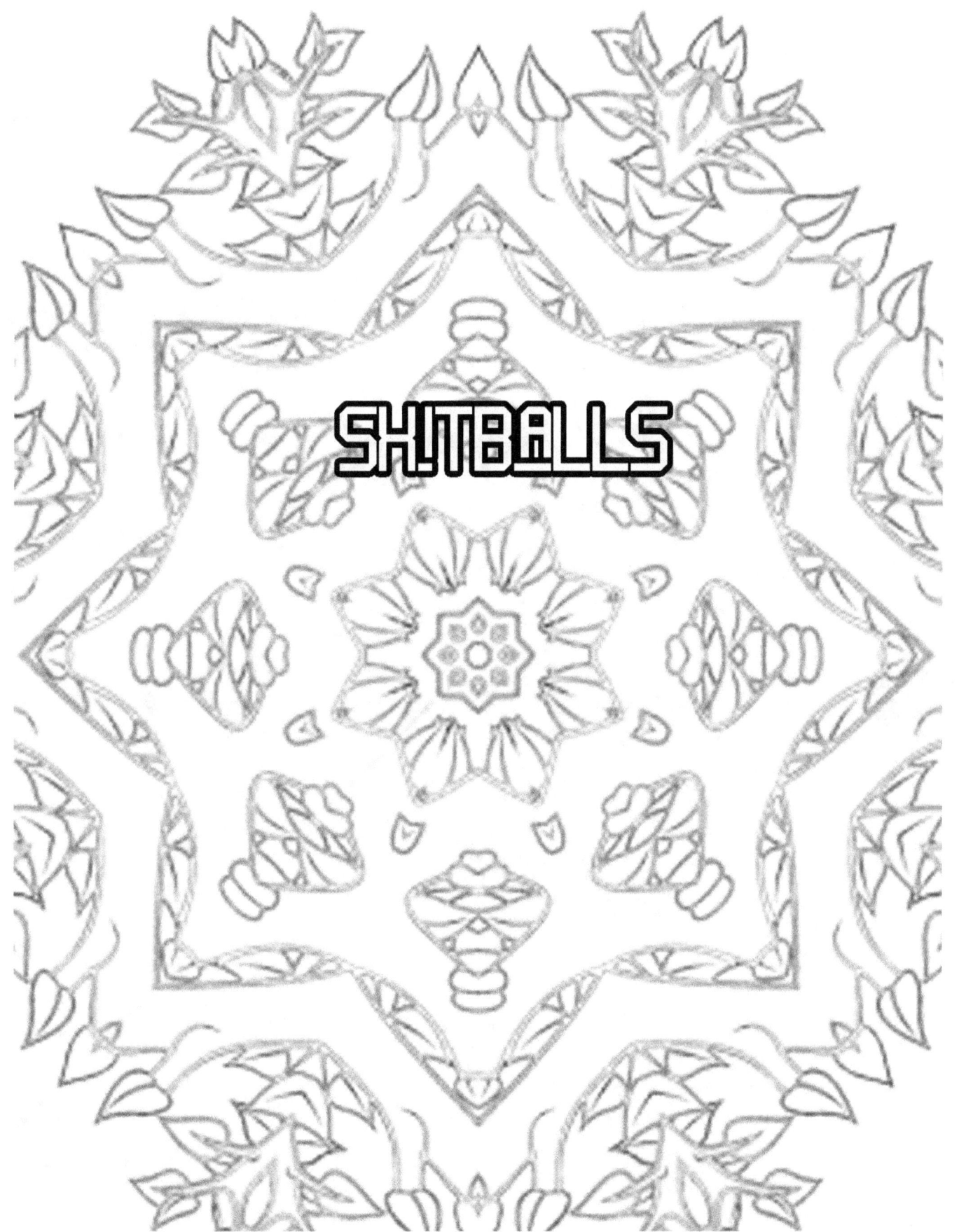

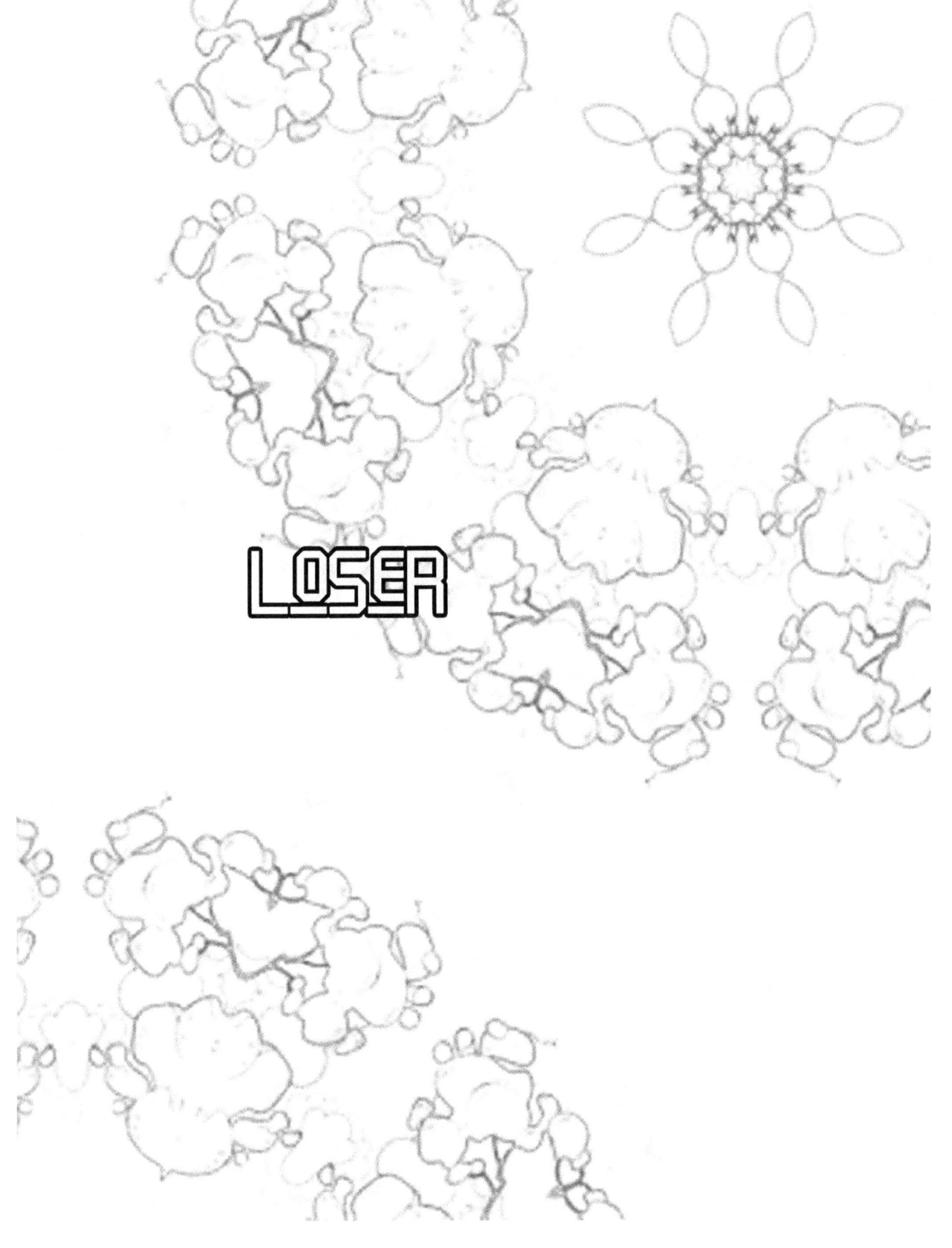

OLD FART

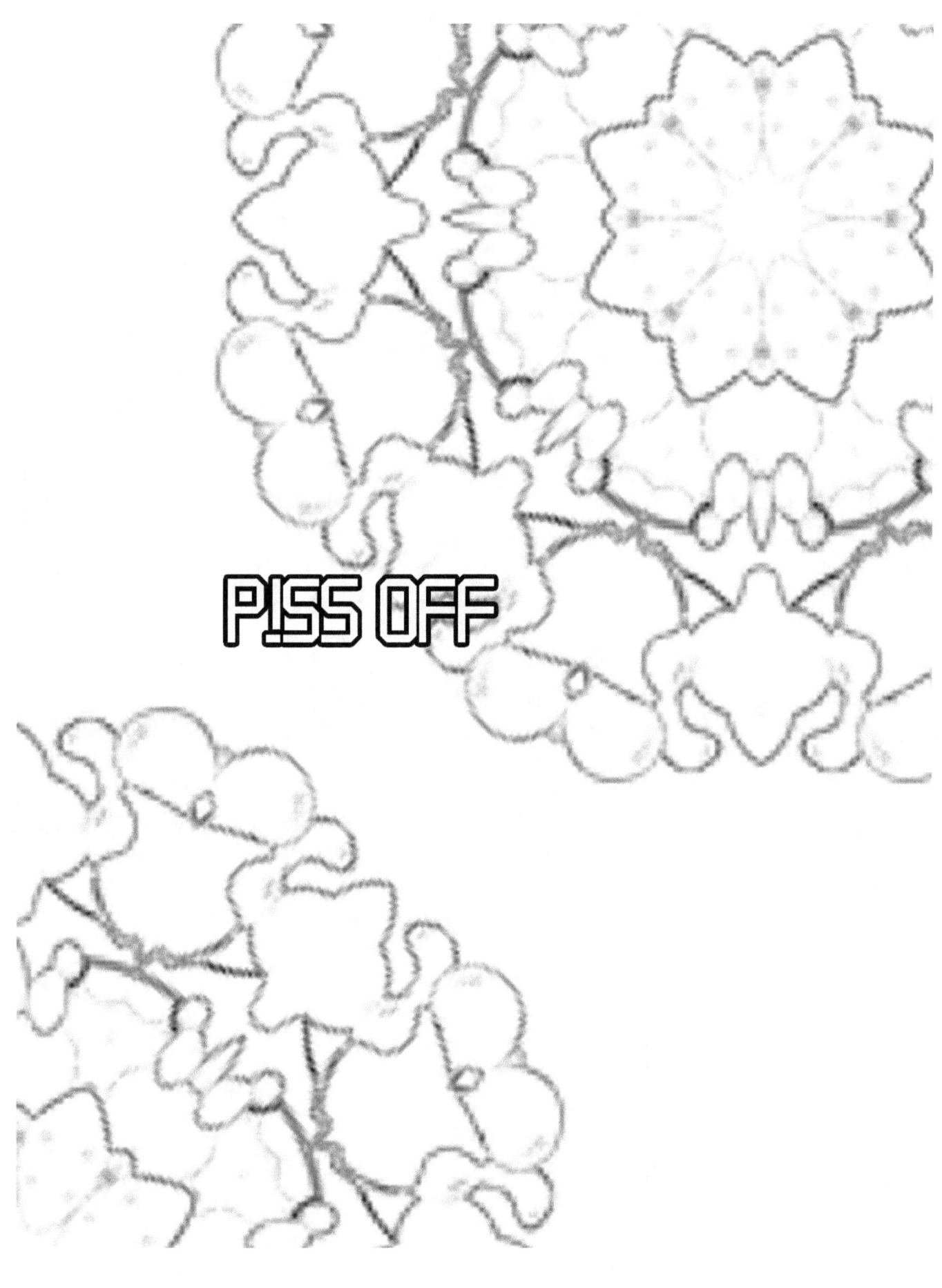

DIPSH!T!D!OT

MORON

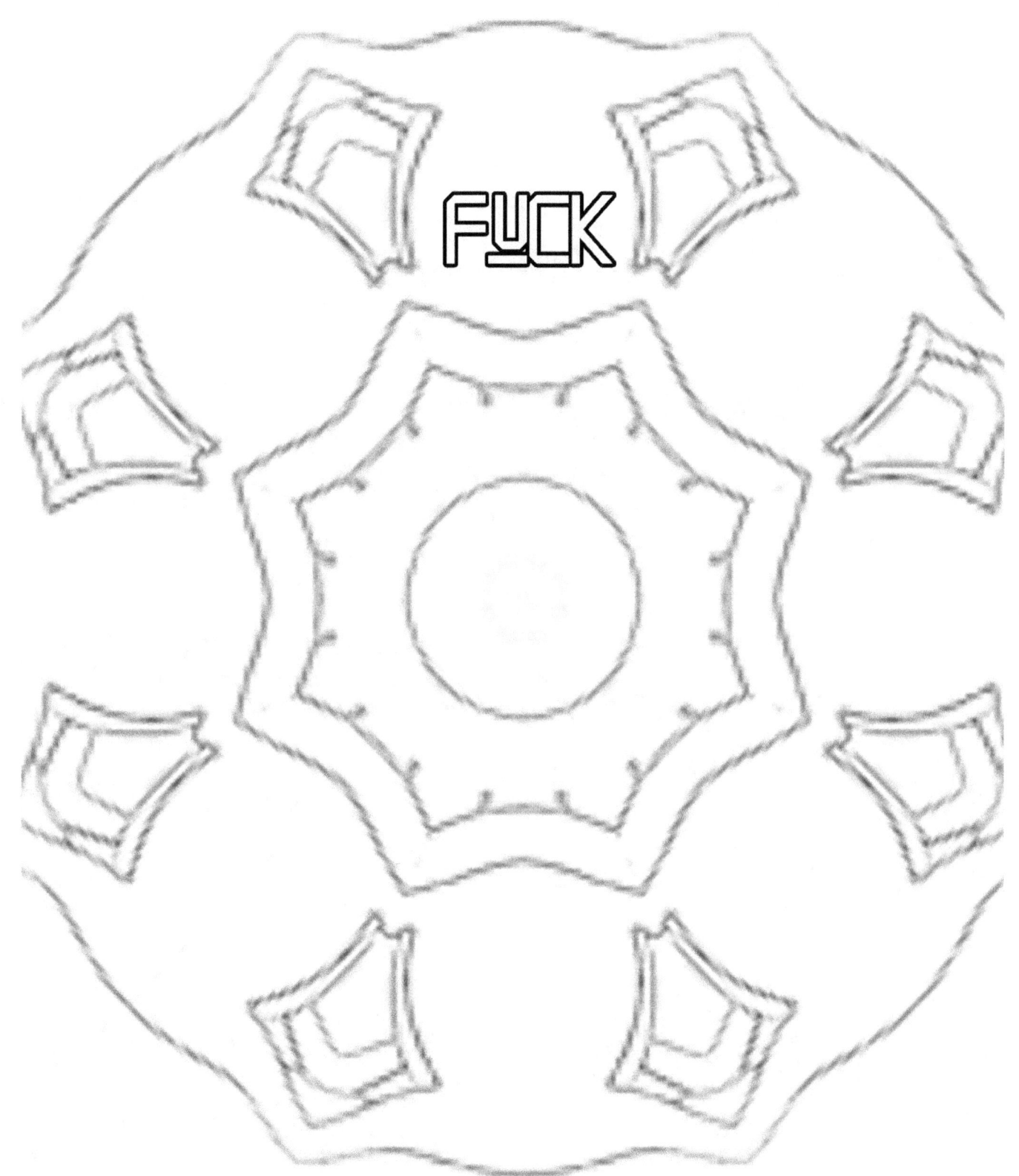

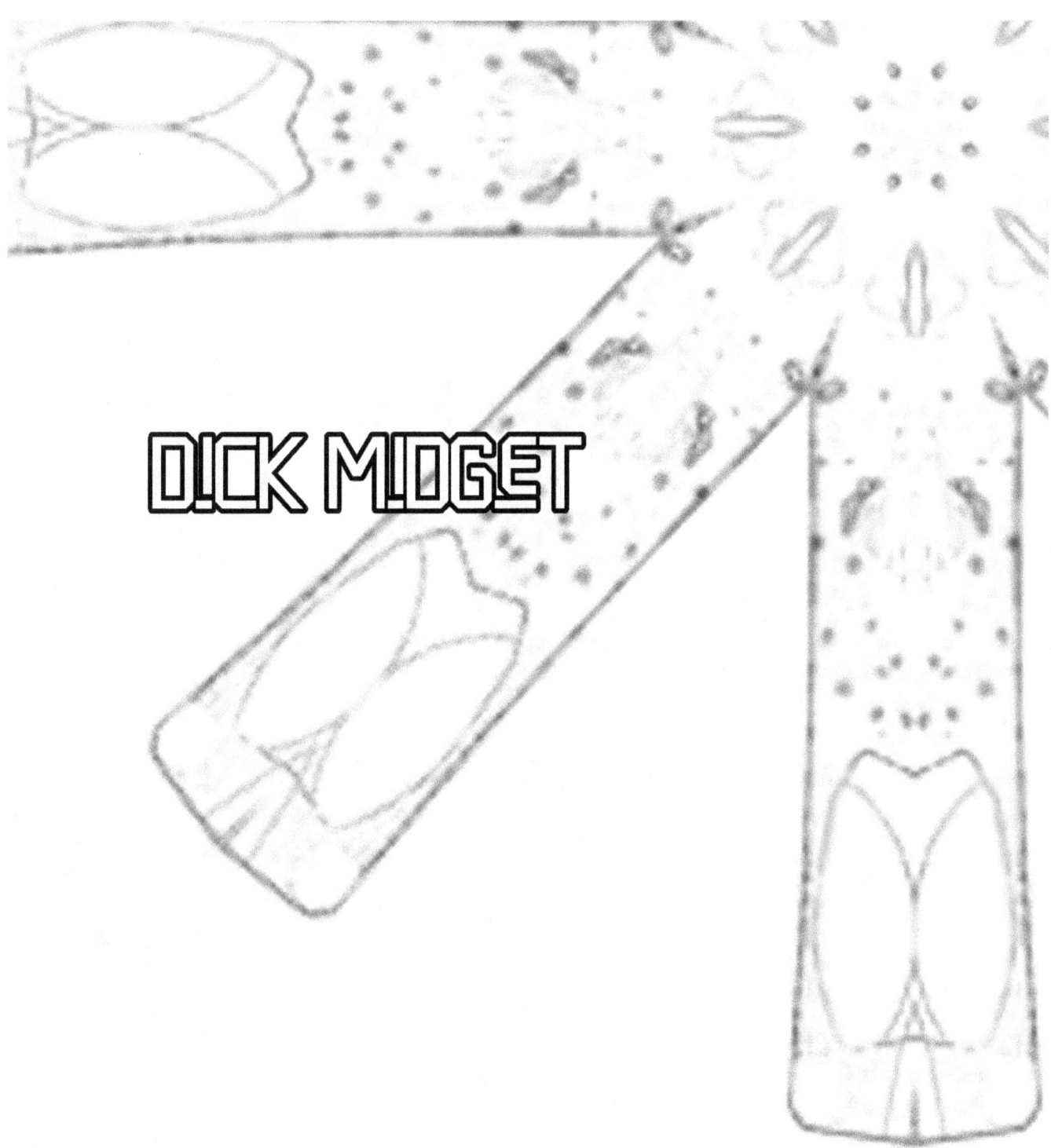

DICK MIDGET

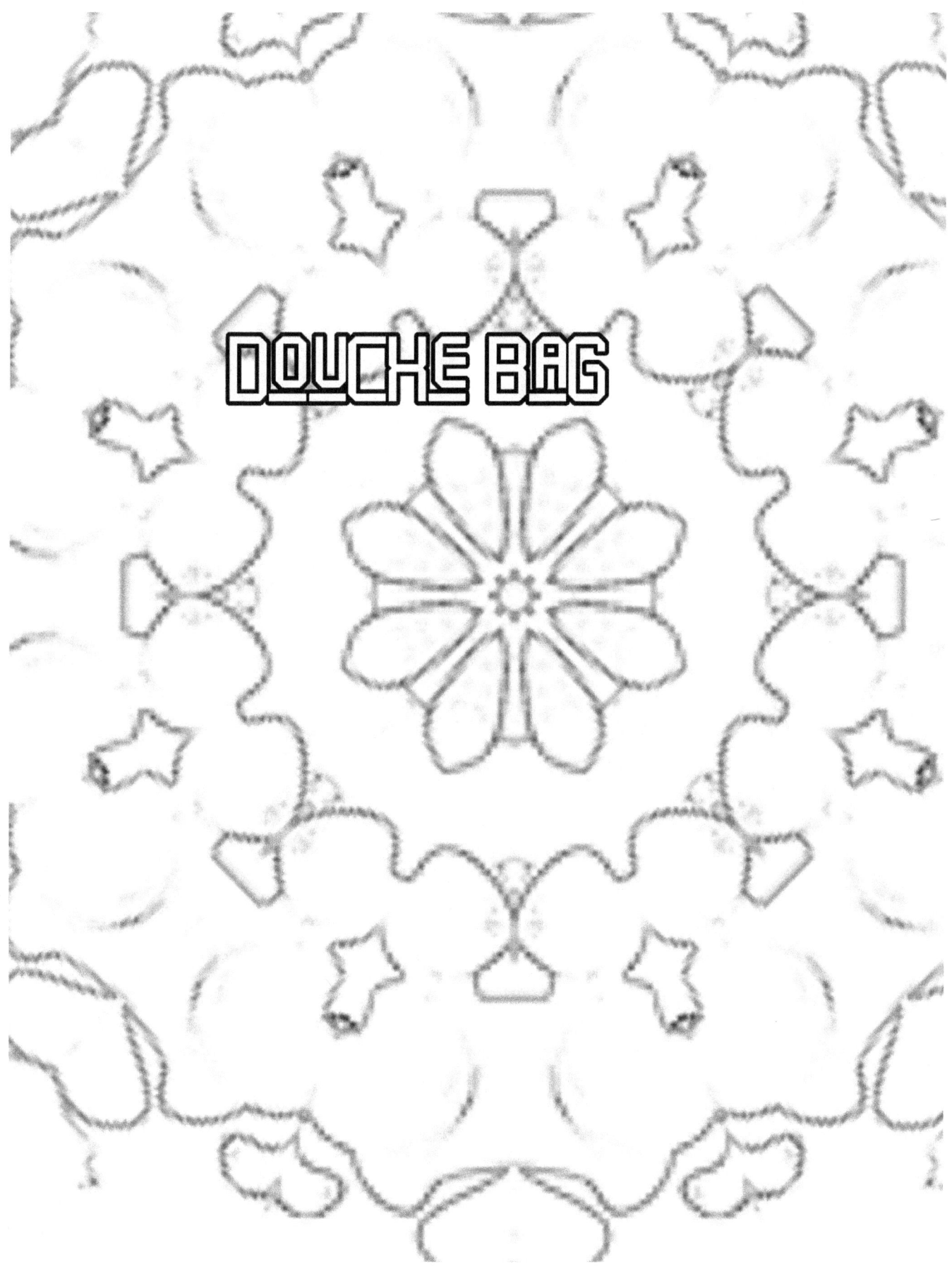

DOUCHE BAG

UGLY BIG SHOES

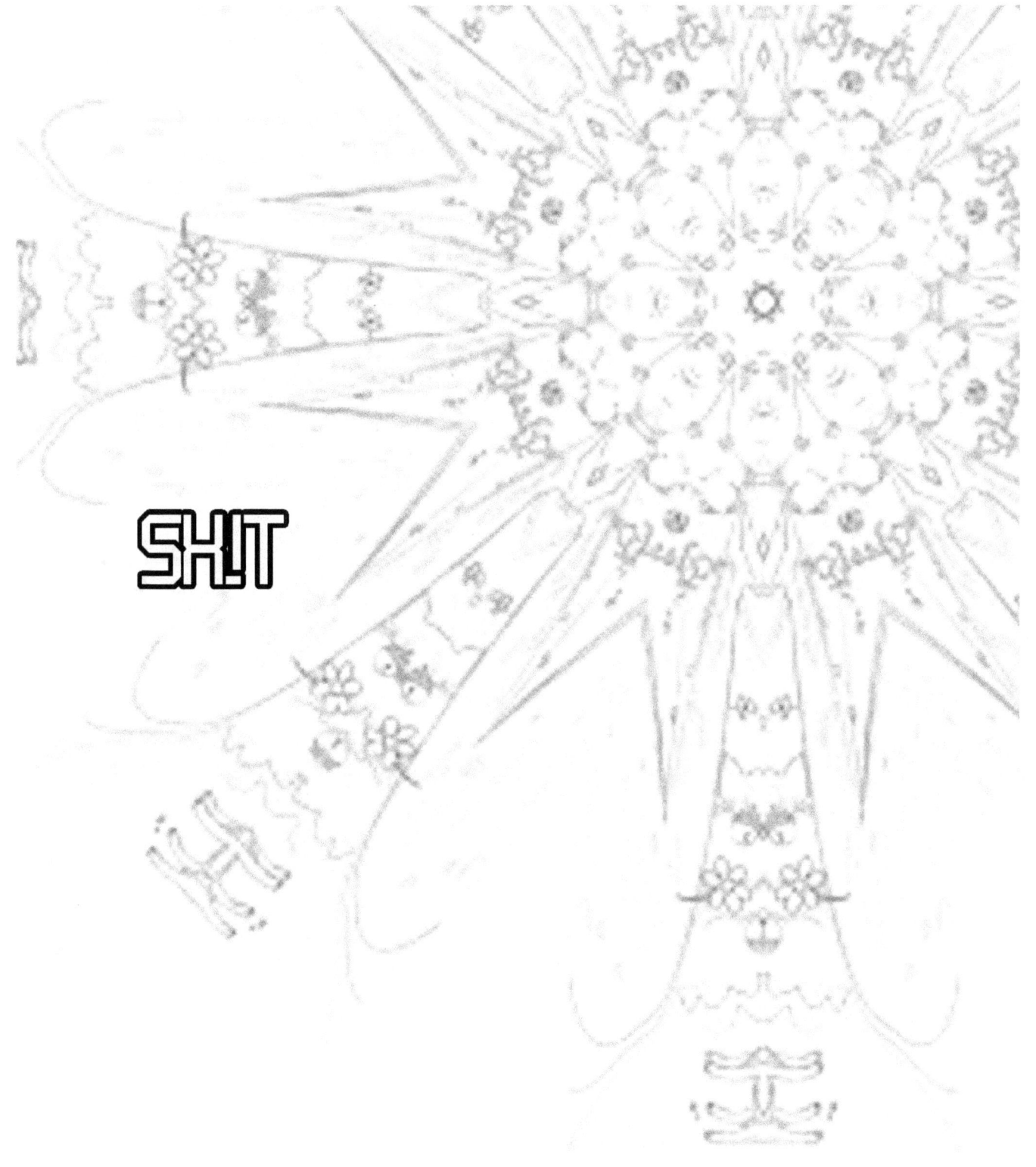

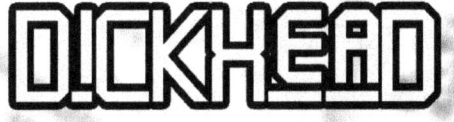

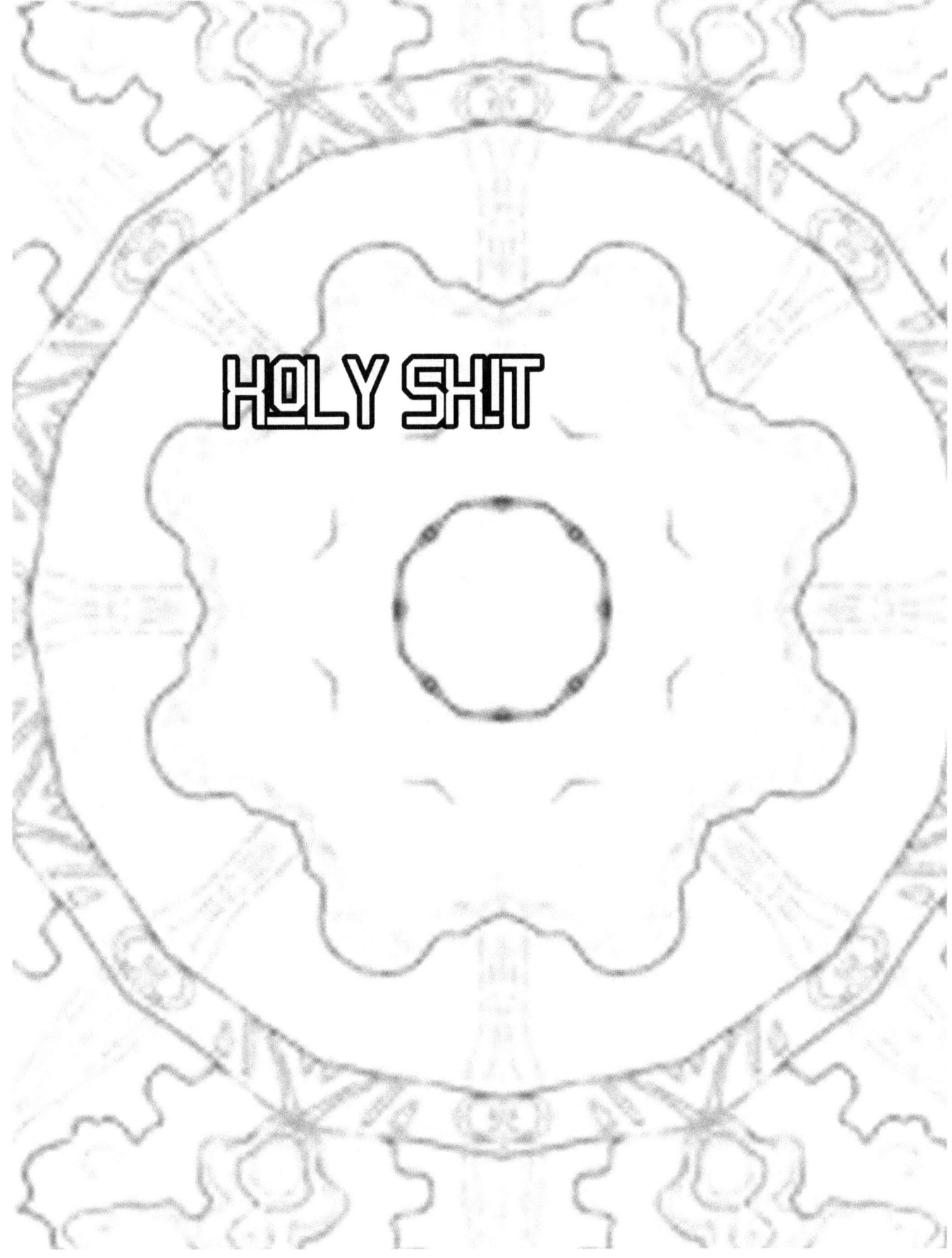

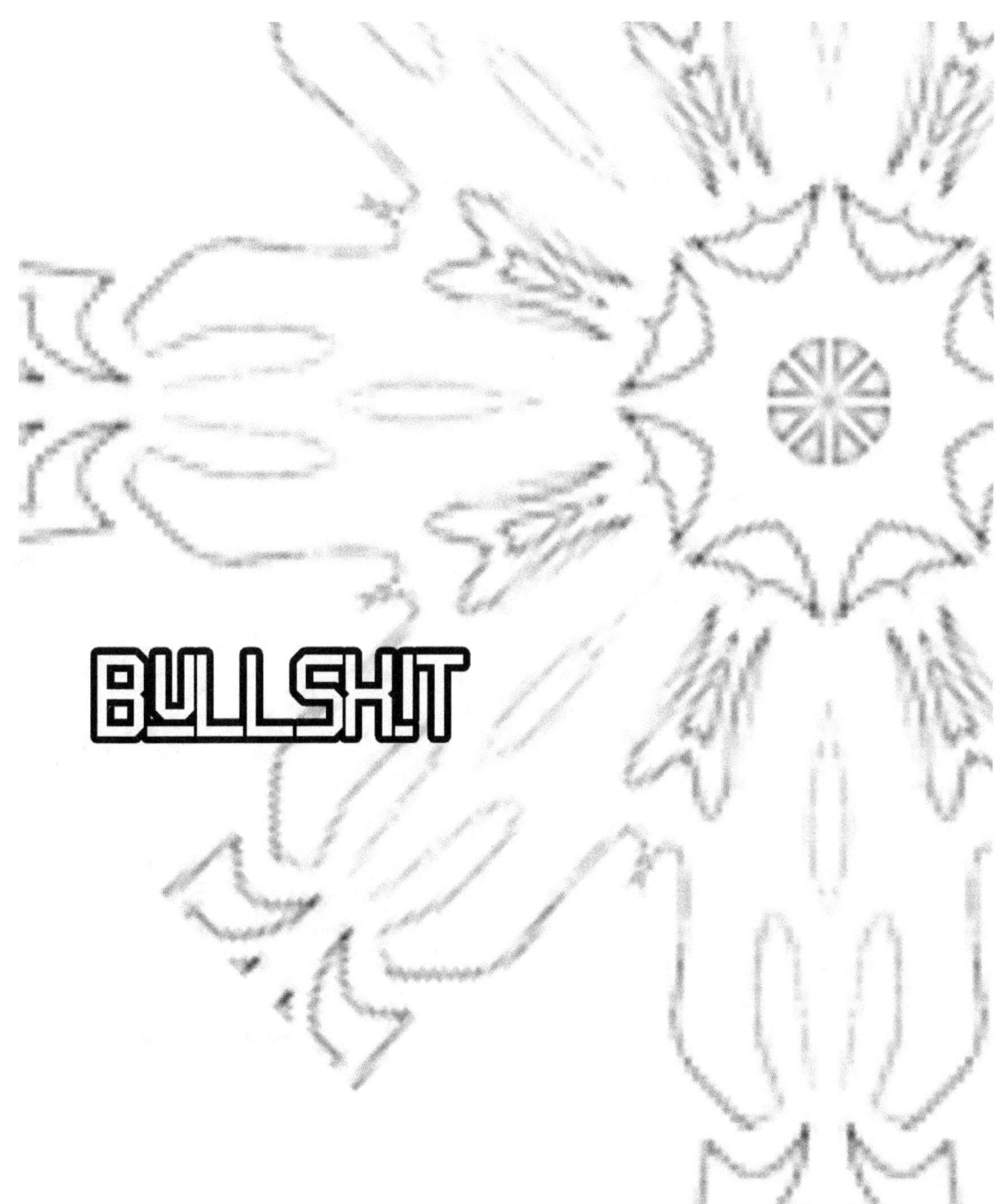

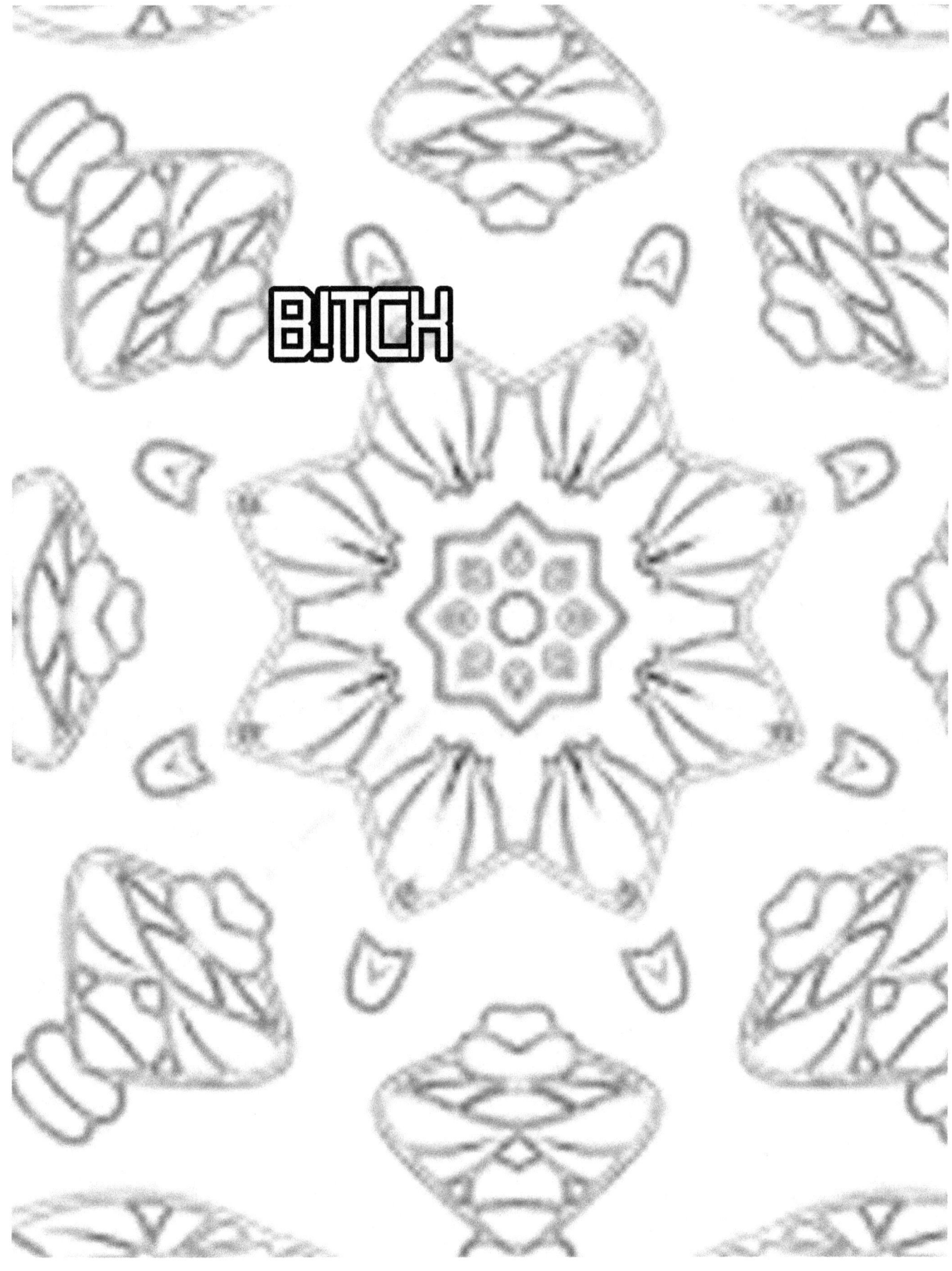

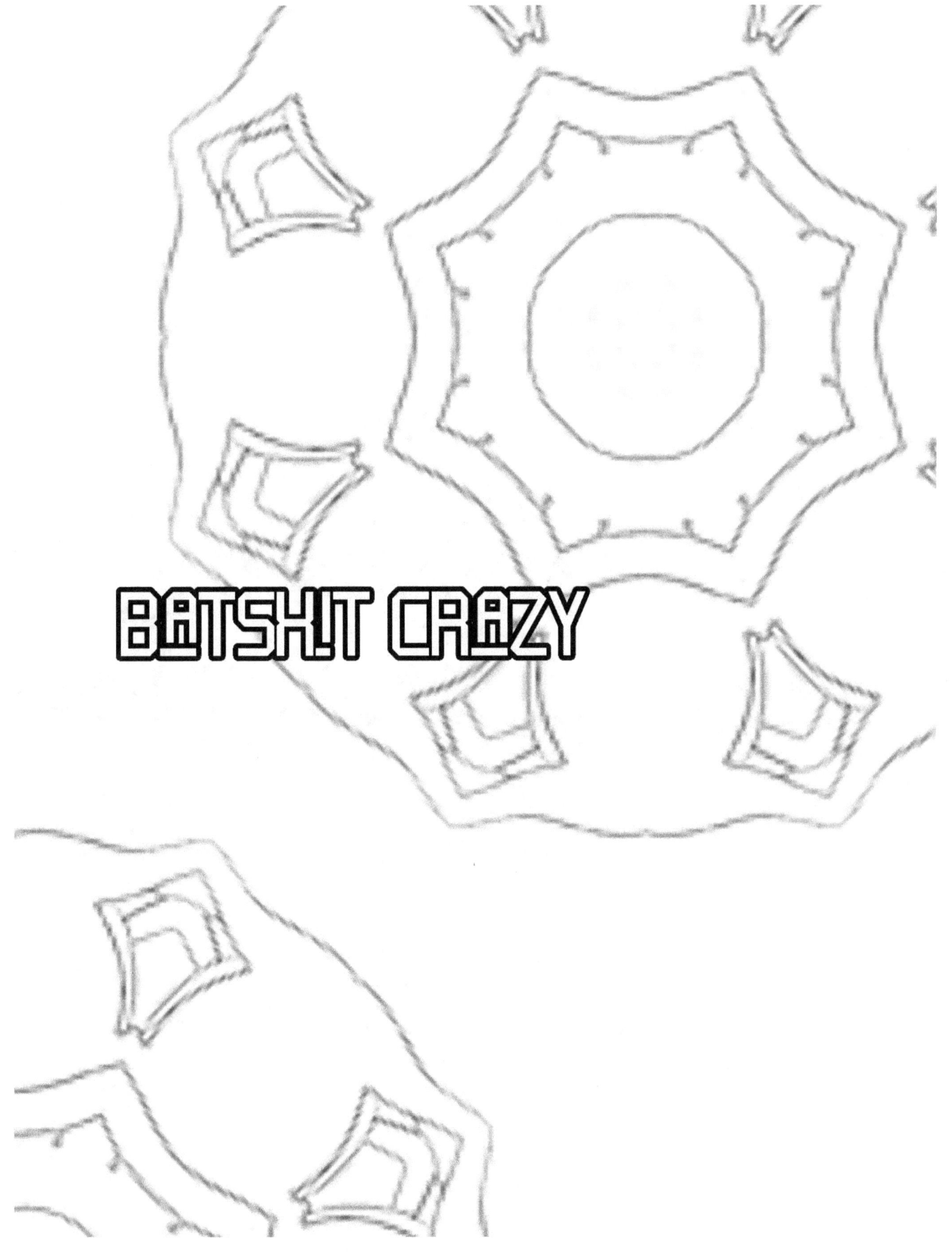

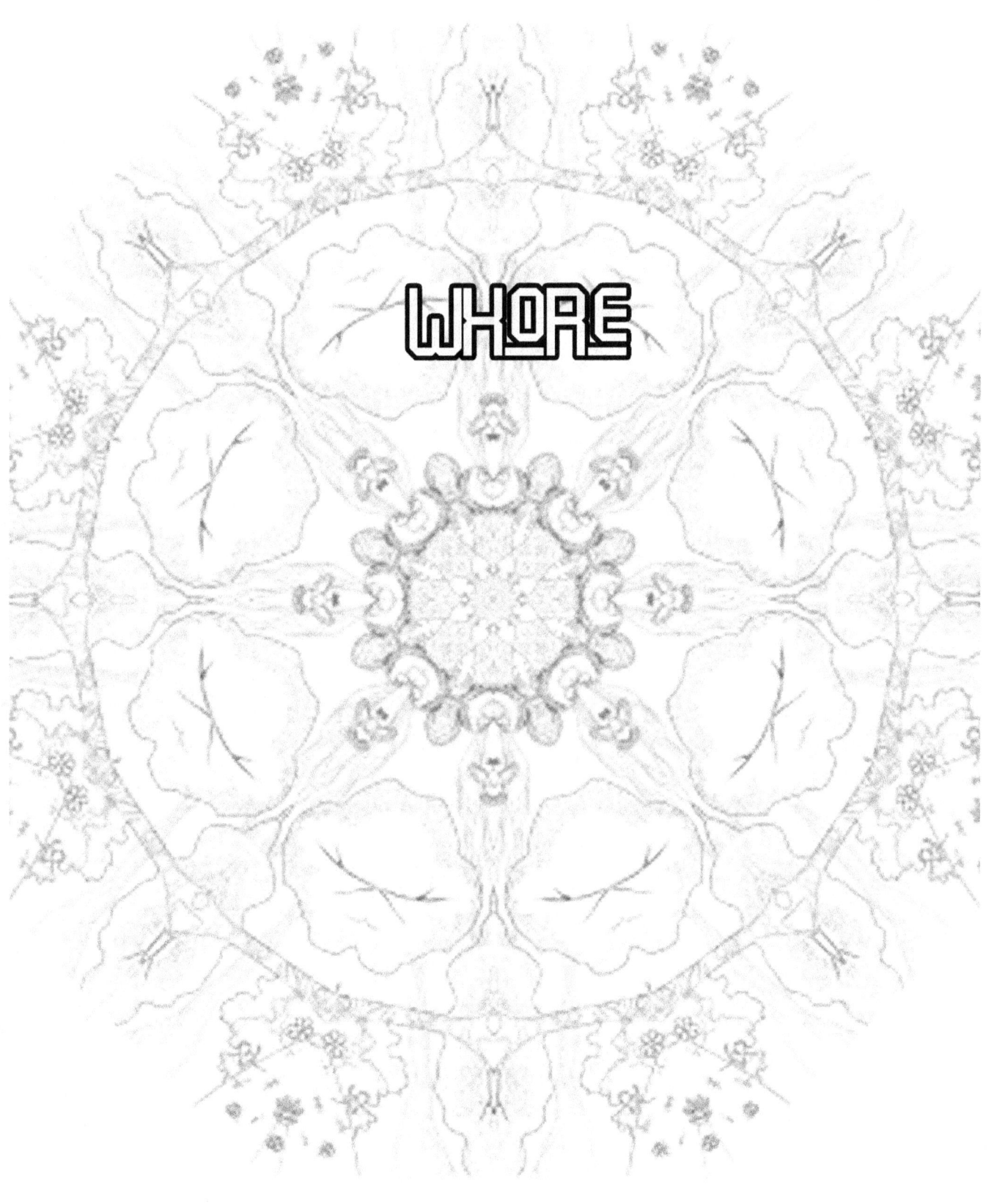

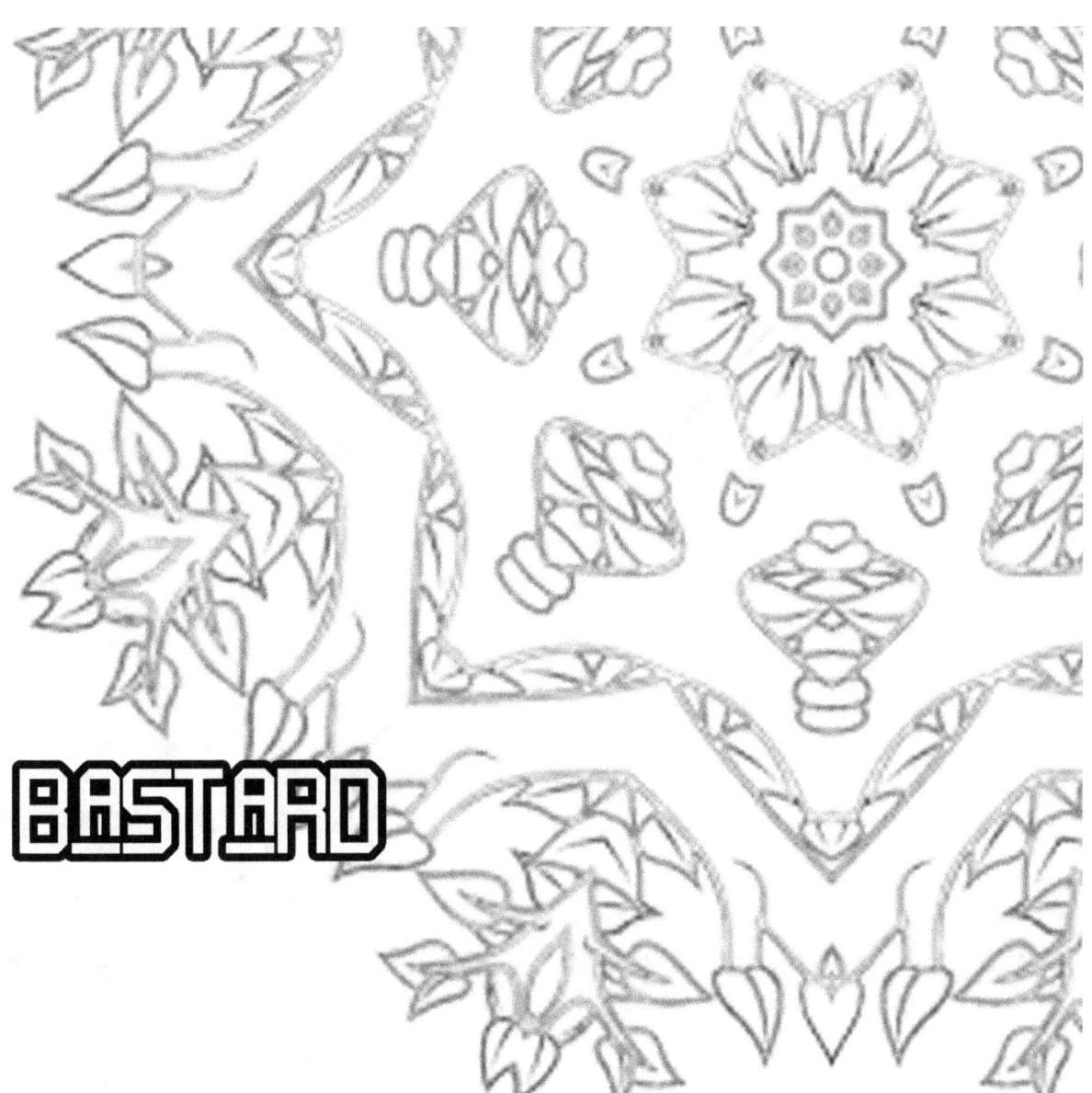

BASTARD

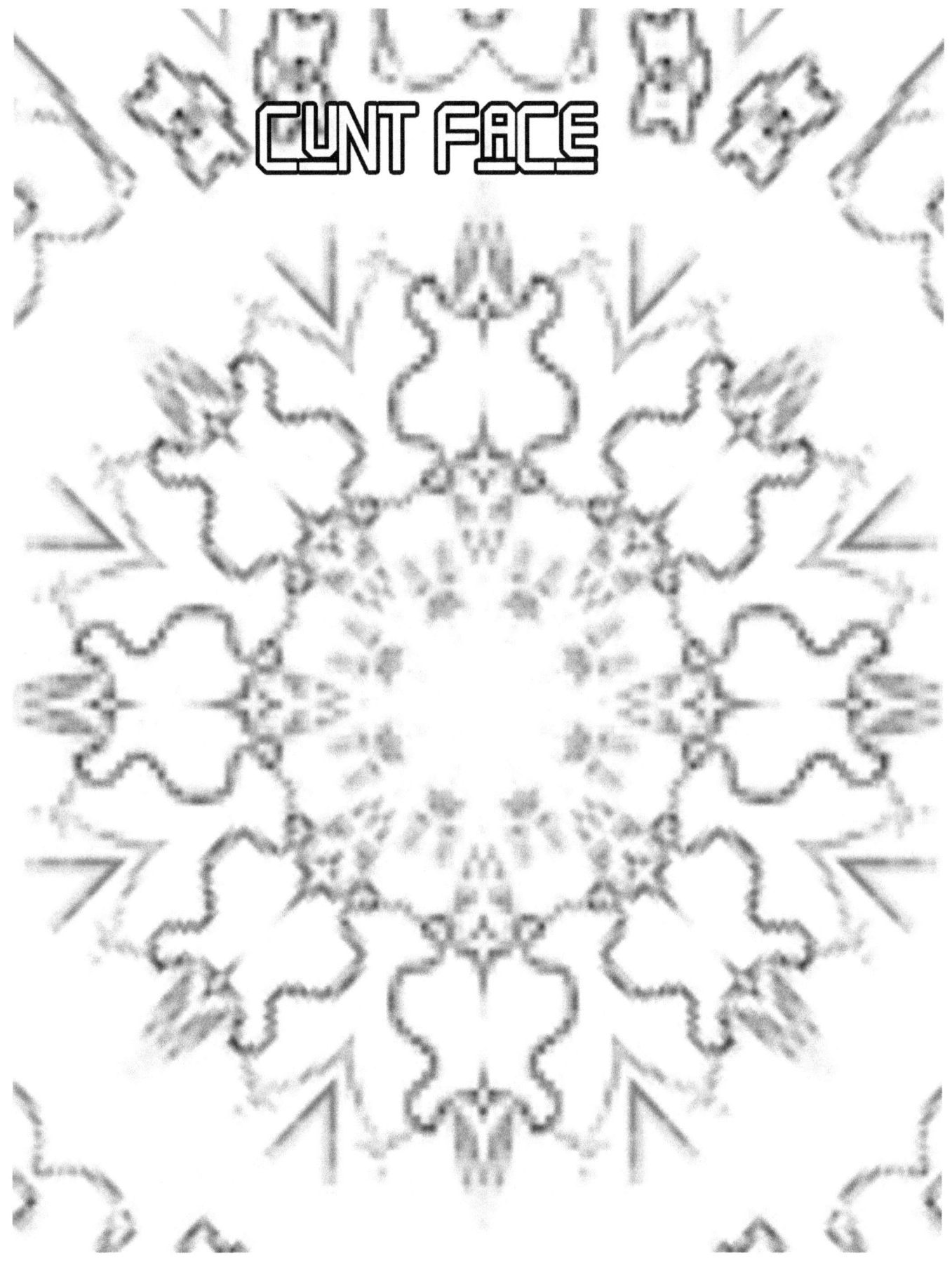

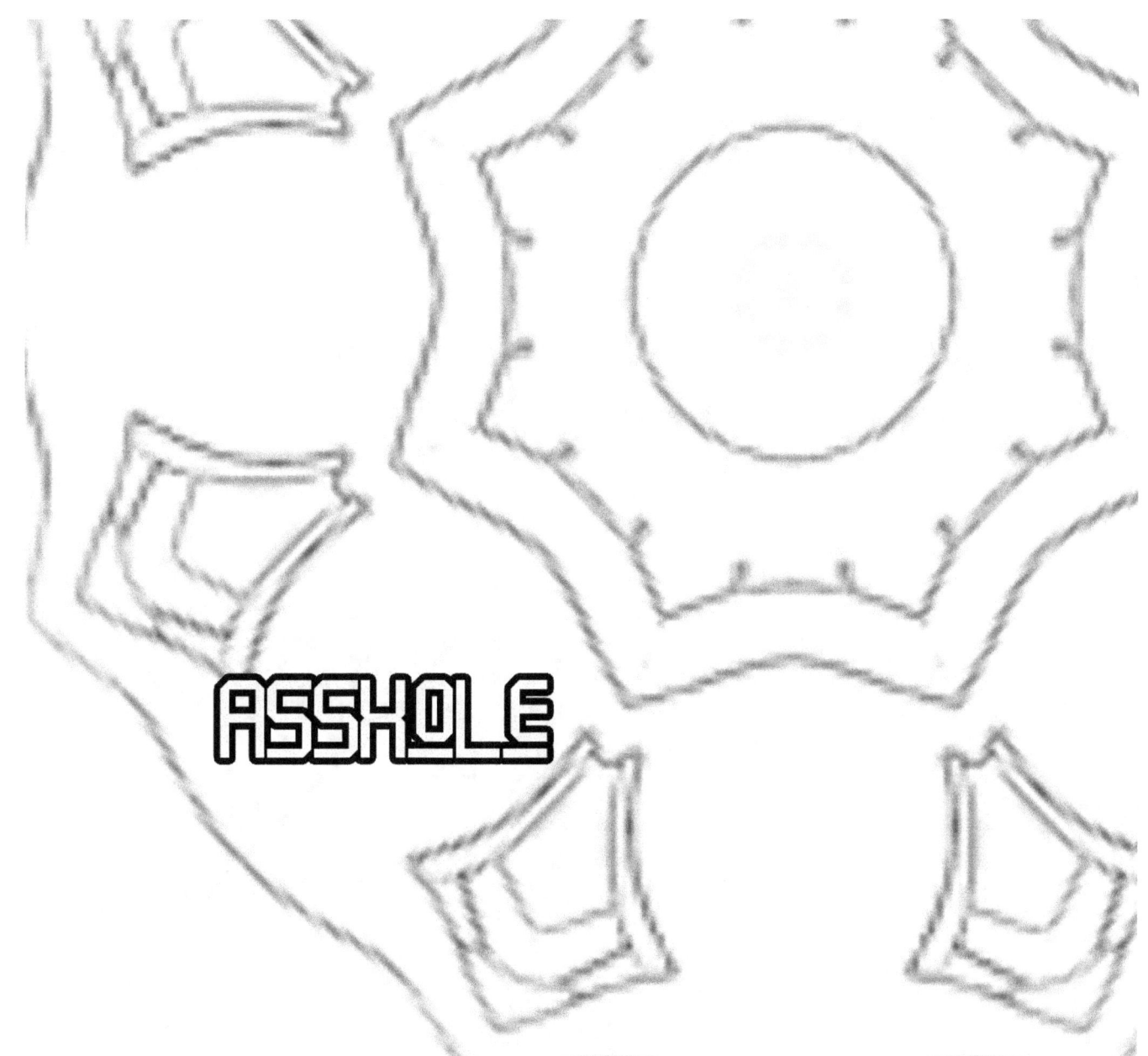

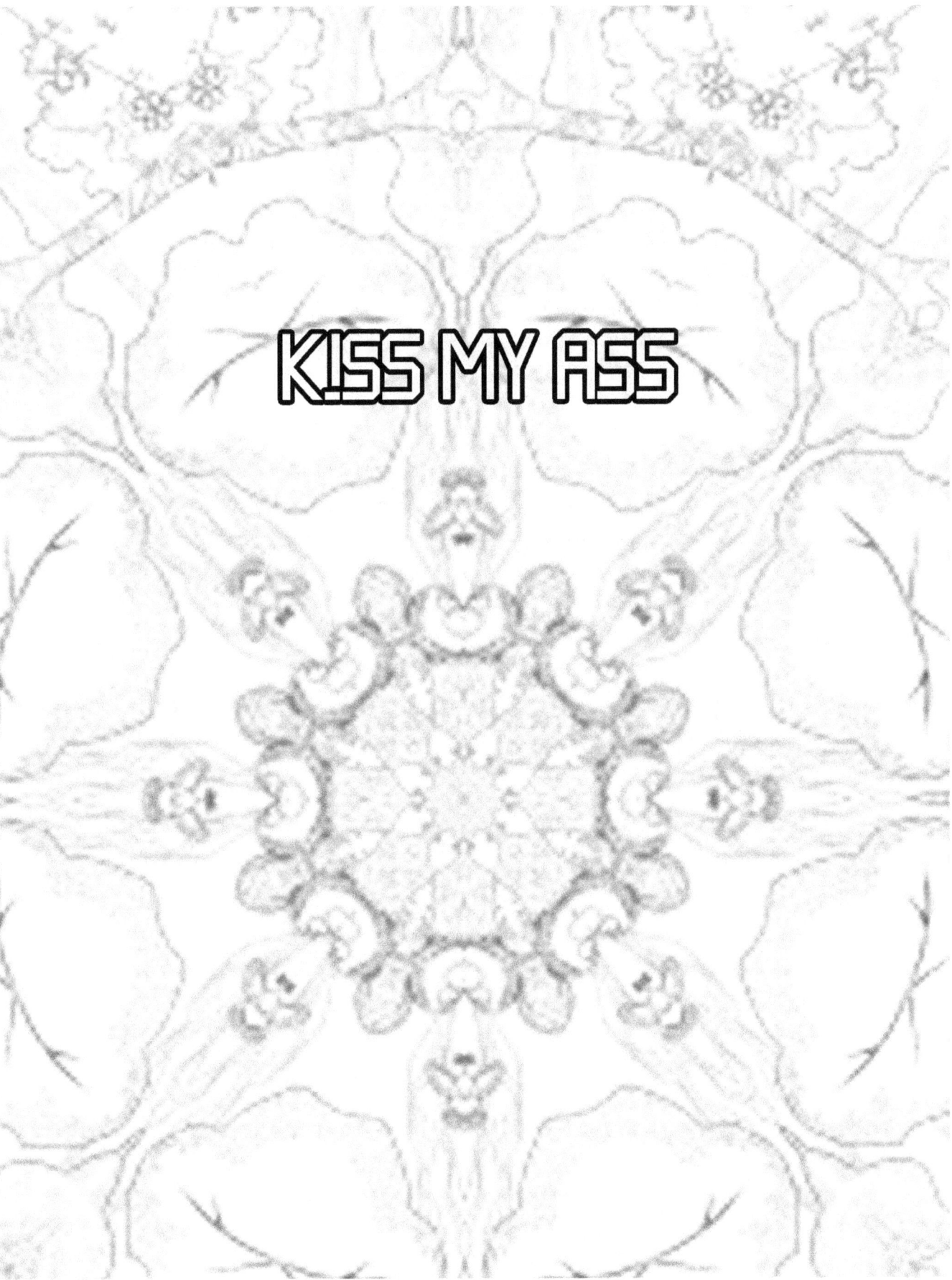

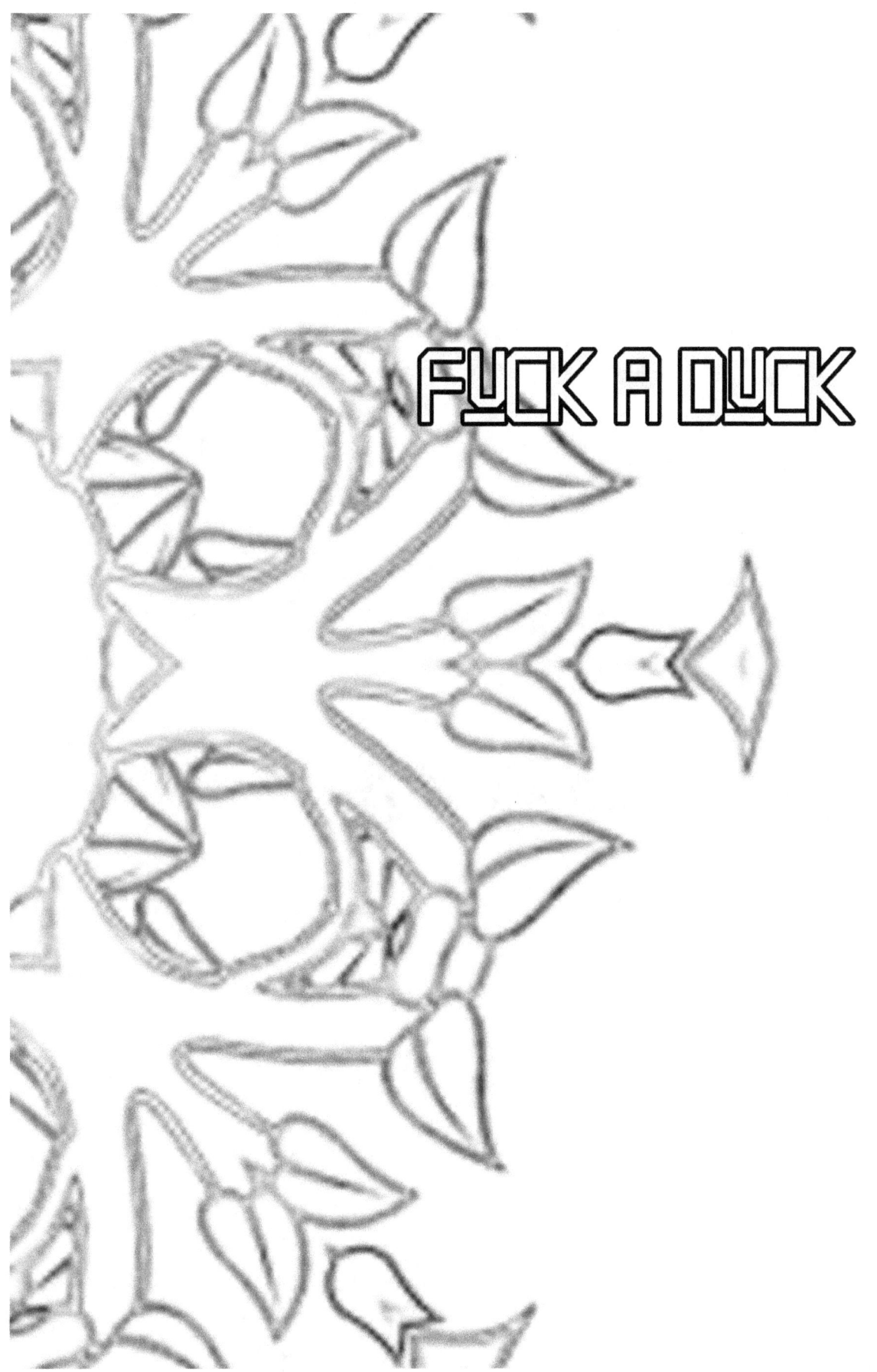

FUCK A DUCK

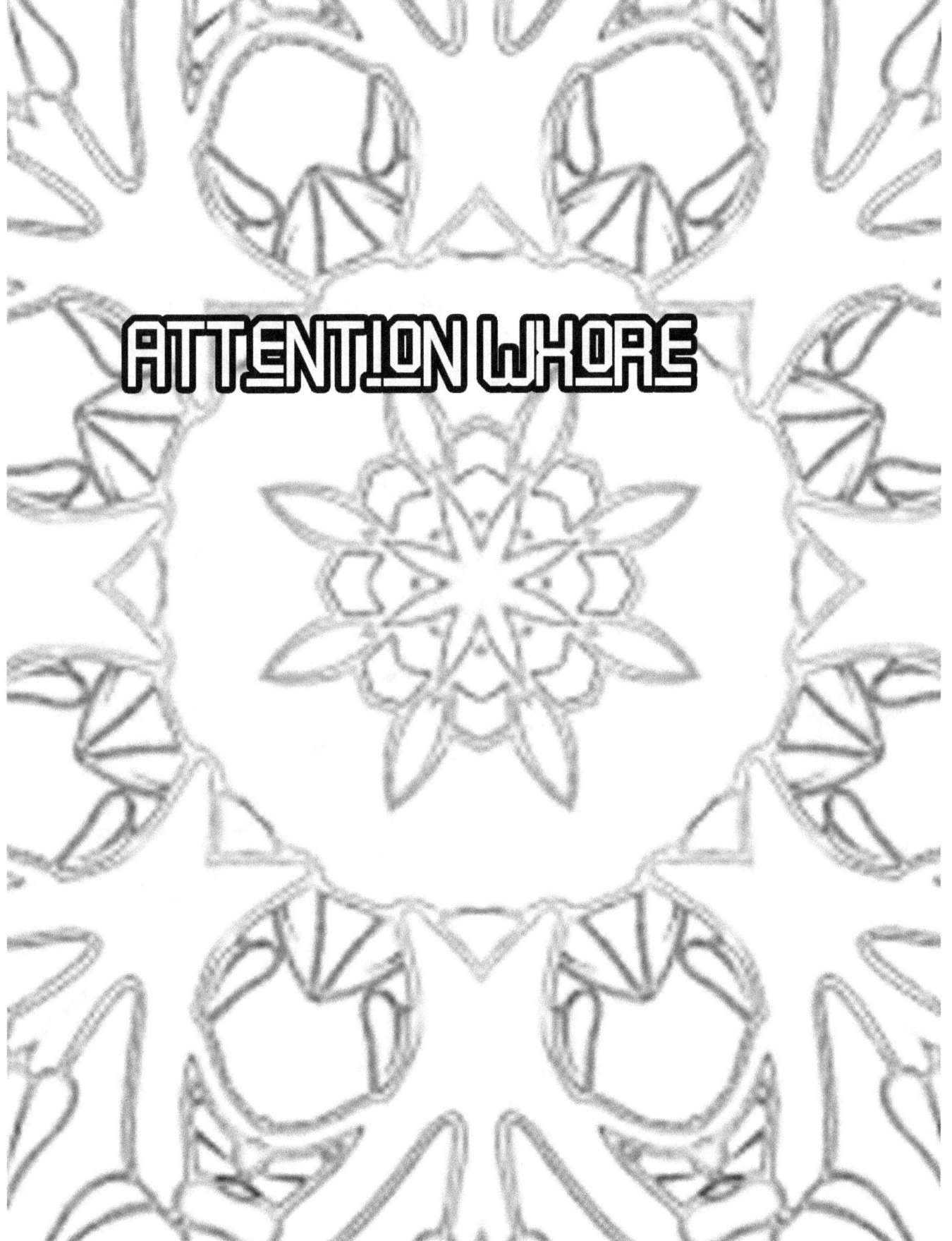

ATTENTION WHORE

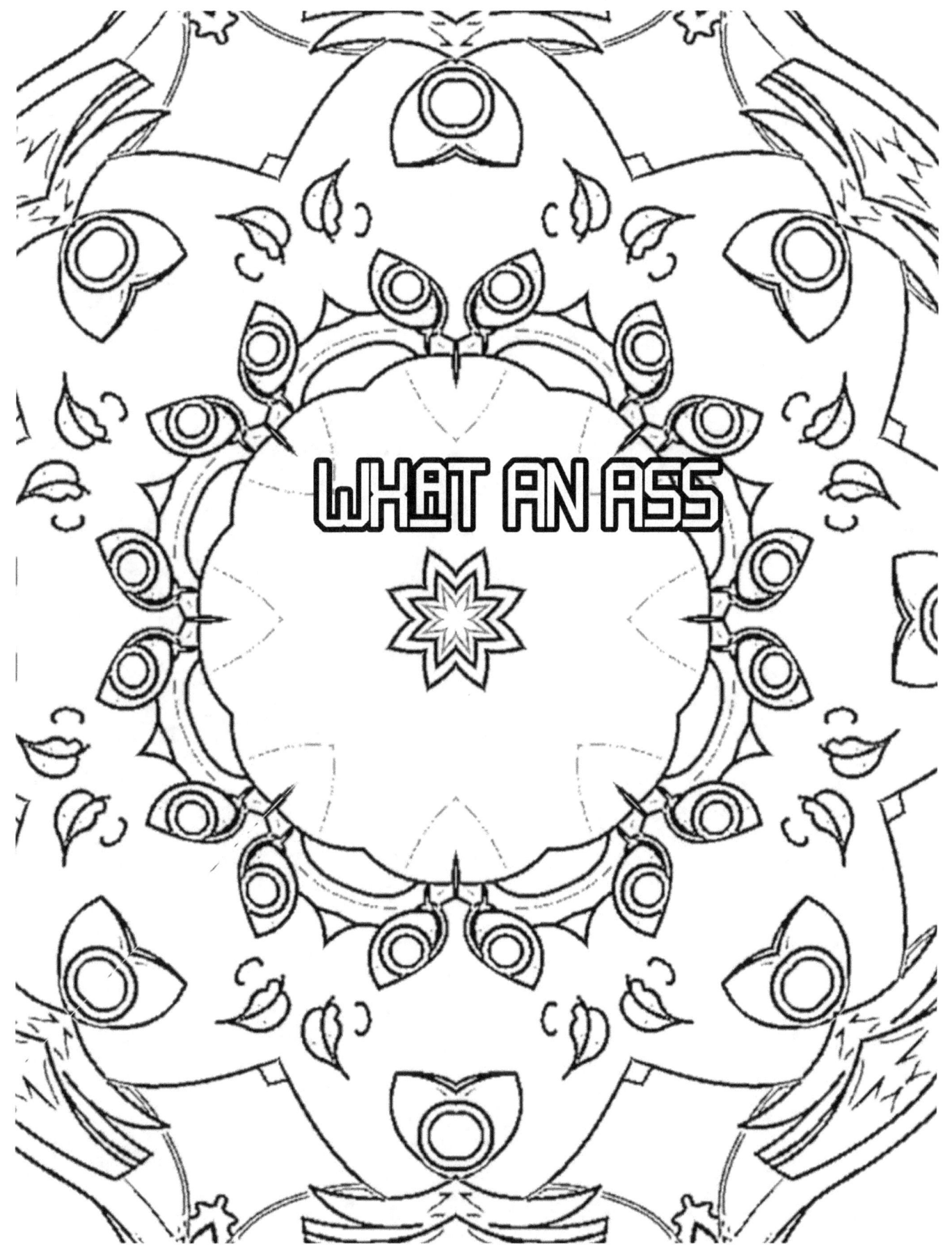

www.ingramcontent.com/pod-product-compliance
Lightning Source LLC
Chambersburg PA
CBHW081747170526
45167CB00009B/3957